WACKY THINGS ABOUT ANIMALS

VOLUME 1

Weird & amazing animal facts!

Written by Tricia Martineau Wagner
Illustrated by Carles Ballesteros

TABLE OF CONTENTS

THE ODD SQUAD

Do you swim inside a shark's mouth for your dinner?
Do you faint when you get scared?

We certainly hope not!

But there are animals that do these and other incredibly wacky things. And you can read all about them right here.

Skunks doing handstands?
Yes.

Tiptoeing horses and
fainting goats?
Why not?!

You'll also discover why these bizarre behaviors are actually perfectly normal for each of these animals. They only seem wacky to us! So prepare for a peculiar parade of vomiting vultures, freezing frogs, and more.

FOOD FOR THOUGHT

Food passes through a giant squid's brain before it makes its way to its stomach. Now that's a brainy idea! The squid has a tiny brain shaped like a doughnut. The *esophagus*, or food tube, runs through the hole. The squid grabs fish with its sharp-hooked tentacles, and its powerful beak tears the fish apart. Then the tiny pieces are fed through the brain.

MORE ABOUT SQUIDS

The colossal squid lives in the deep, cold waters around the southern tip of Africa down to Antarctica. The cold temperatures make the squid digest food slowly so it does not need much food. Colossal squids weigh up to 1,600 pounds (725 kilograms) and can grow up to 46 feet (14 meters) long. That's longer than a school bus!

LAZY BIRDS

If you were not related to a cuckoo bird, you would end up doing all of its chores! Cuckoo birds are so lazy that they don't even raise their own children. Instead, female cuckoos lay their eggs in other birds' nests. And even though the baby cuckoo hatchlings look nothing like the other baby birds in the nest, their new parents still care for them.

MORE ABOUT CUCKOO BIRDS

Cuckoo birds live in Europe, Africa, Asia, and Australia. A newly hatched cuckoo bird will often try to push the unhatched eggs out of the nest so it can eat more of the food. Yet each year, different birds accept cuckoo eggs in their nests.

SCAREDY GOATS

If someone comes up behind you and yells "boo!," your muscles will tense up for a moment. If you scare a Tennessee Fainting Goat, the same thing happens... except it's much worse. As the goat begins to run away, its muscles completely freeze up, and it falls on its back or side. After about ten seconds, the goat can get up and move around again.

MORE ABOUT TENNESSEE FAINTING GOATS

These goats aren't actually fainting—they just lose their ability to run as their muscles freeze up. This condition isn't too much of a problem on a farm, but they wouldn't last long in the wild!

STINKY DANCERS

This silly sight should give you a fright! When a spotted skunk feels trouble is near, it will stand on its front paws, dance, and wave its tail. This isn't so you will die laughing—the handstand makes the skunk looks bigger and more dangerous. If a predator isn't smart enough to heed this warning, the skunk will squirt a stinky spray that can cause temporary blindness and nausea.

MORE ABOUT SPOTTED SKUNKS

The spotted skunk lives in the southern half of North America. The skunk's spray sac gives off five squirts, and it takes about a week to produce new spray. That's why they dance first, and spray only if they are in real danger.

TIPPY TOES

Can you win a race running on your tippy toes? Horses do! Each foot has a single large toe and two smaller toes, and the smaller toes don't touch the ground when the horse runs. They are connected to the big toe and give it support to prevent the horse from twisting its foot while running.

MORE ABOUT HORSES

Horse's toes are covered by a thick, tough toenail called a *hoof*. The hoof makes contact with the ground. Horses need to have their hooves trimmed often. Special instruments called hoof nippers and rasps are used to clip and file the hooves.

COW MAGNETS

Lost? Well, you don't need a compass to find north and south. Just locate some hungry cows! Earth's magnetic poles make a compass needle point north and south. But the poles seem to make cows' heads turn as well. When eating or resting, cows line up in a north-south direction according to Earth's magnetic field. And they swivel their heads north or south when grazing.

MORE ABOUT COWS

Scientists used satellite images to look down on cattle from high above Earth. They studied 8,000 head of cattle around the world. Scientists also discovered that deer do the same thing when grazing or resting.

POTTY MOUTH

If you see a Chinese soft-shelled turtle spitting, it's probably not water. This turtle pees through its mouth. Eww! Peeing the normal way takes a lot of water, and since these turtles live in salty water that they can't drink, they need to conserve water any way they can. To clean their mouth, all they have to do is rinse with the salty water and spit.

MORE ABOUT CHINESE SOFT-SHELL TURTLES

This turtle is the only known animal that pees this way. It lives in and around China, and has also been introduced to other countries, including the United States. It is found in rivers, lakes, ponds, creeks, canals, and marshes.

FREEZING FROGS

Can you imagine freezing during the cold winter and thawing out in the warm spring? That is exactly what the North American wood frog does! It survives winter with more than half of its body's water turned to ice. The frog buries itself underground and goes into a deep hibernation for two to three months. During winter, the wood frog's breathing and heartbeat stop, but it doesn't die.

MORE ABOUT NORTH AMERICAN WOOD FROGS

The North American wood frog is one of the few frogs that can survive in Alaska and above the Arctic Circle. When frozen, the frog's body temperature ranges from 21 to 30 degrees Fahrenheit (-6 to -1 degrees Celsius). Come spring, the frog warms up and its heart starts beating again.

BIG BABY BINKY

An elephant uses its trunk for smelling, breathing, squirting water, feeding itself, picking up objects, and exploring its environment. Elephants even use their trunks to hug each other. But baby elephants, called *calves*, suck their trunks when they are scared, cranky, or tired. They may weigh 200 pounds (100 kilograms), but they need comfort just like human babies do.

MORE ABOUT ELEPHANTS

There are two types of elephants: the Asian elephant and the African elephant. African elephants are the largest land mammals. An elephant's trunk has 100,000 muscles, can grow up to 6 feet long (2 meters), and can weigh up to 308 pounds (140 kilograms).

TURTLE TEARS

Butterflies spend a lot of time hovering around yellow spotted river turtles. What do they want? Turtle tears! The fluid that wells up in these turtles' eyes is salty. Since the butterflies need that salt to live, they excitedly swarm around the turtles' heads to sip the tears.

MORE ABOUT YELLOW SPOTTED RIVER TURTLES

Yellow spotted river turtles live in the Amazon rain forest. These meat-eating turtles get all the salt they need from their diet. The butterflies, however, don't get enough salt from their diet of plant nectar. That's why they go after the turtle tears. Scientists don't think this process hurts the turtles, but they aren't 100-percent sure yet.

DUST BUSTER

If you're ever caught in a desert sandstorm, you better have your goggles with you. Otherwise you'll be blinded by blowing sand. Camels, on the other hand, are always prepared. Camels have thick eyebrows and really long eyelashes. They can clamp their long eyelashes together to create a shield over their eyes to keep out all the dust!

MORE ABOUT CAMELS

Camels also have three eyelids. The third eyelid can be closed during a sandstorm as extra protection. Camel's humps are made out of body fat that can be turned to water or energy.

ALL PUFFED UP

Pufferfish should be an easy meal for predators. (They are slow, clumsy swimmers.) But they have a clever way of scaring away enemies. Pufferfish suck in water and blow themselves up to several times their original size. Suddenly, what looked like a good meal is now a giant, scary water balloon with eyes and fins. They can stay inflated for 15 minutes, then they need to rest for five hours afterward.

MORE ABOUT PUFFERFISH

Pufferfish live mostly in tropical and subtropical waters. They are extremely poisonous. But that doesn't stop trained chefs from removing the poisonous parts and preparing *fugu*, a tasty (but risky) Japanese dish.

VULTURE VOMIT

Look out if vultures feel threatened! Vultures feed on *carcasses*, or dead animal bodies. This helps clean up roadkill on streets and highways. But any predator coming after a vulture while it's eating is in for a surprise. The vulture will vomit in the direction of the enemy. Emptying its stomach lightens it, so it can quickly fly away.

MORE ABOUT VULTURES

Vultures do not have strong feet or beaks, so they can't carry food back to their nests for their hungry offspring. Therefore, vultures eat food and regurgitate, or throw up, the food to feed their young.

FISH FLOSSERS

Would you swim inside a shark's mouth? Most fish swim far away when sharks come around, but pilot fish don't! Pilot fish actually swim inside a shark's mouth, and act as a shark toothbrush. They never have to worry about becoming the shark's next meal because the shark leaves the fish alone in return for the teeth cleaning.

MORE ABOUT PILOT FISH

Pilot fish nibble away at food particles stuck between sharks' teeth. They also eat harmful parasites that would make the sharks sick. When not darting in and out of a shark's mouth, pilot fish swim underneath the shark, making it difficult for other predators to catch them.

This library edition published in 2018 by Walter Foster Jr.,
an imprint of The Quarto Group
26391 Crown Valley Parkway, Suite 220
Mission Viejo, CA 92691, USA.

© 2017 Quarto Publishing Group USA Inc.
Published by Walter Foster Jr.,
an imprint of The Quarto Group
All rights reserved. Walter Foster Jr. is trademarked.

Written by Tricia Martineau Wagner
Illustrated by Carles Ballesteros

Distributed in the United States and Canada by
Lerner Publisher Services
241 First Avenue North
Minneapolis, MN 55401 U.S.A.
www.lernerbooks.com

First Library Edition

  Library of Congress Cataloging-in-Publication Data

Names: Wagner, Tricia Martineau, author. | Ballesteros, Carles, illustrator.
Title: Wacky things about animals : weird & amazing animal facts! / written
    by Tricia Martineau Wagner ; illustrated by Carles Ballesteros.
Description: First library edition. | Lake Forest, CA : Walter Foster Jr., an
    imprint of The Quarto Group, 2018. | Audience: Age 7+ | Audience: Grade 4
    to 6.
Identifiers: LCCN 2018009315| ISBN 9781942875697 (hardcover : volume 1) |
    ISBN 9781942875703 (hardcover : volume 2)
Subjects: LCSH: Animals--Juvenile literature.
Classification: LCC QL49 .W185 2018 | DDC 590--dc23
LC record available at https://lccn.loc.gov/2018009315

Printed in USA
9 8 7 6 5 4 3 2

Also available in this series:

9781942875703

9781600587887

9781600587894